Emotional Forest

A Journey of A Man, Giving
A Brother The Permission
to Express Himself.

By

Draevious Bivens

Published by Millennial Invasion.

ISBN: 9781955297288

Acknowledgments

I would like to thank these individuals who believed in me before my project was even done. As the process got a little rough, y'all were the ones that kept me going with y'all support. So to y'all, I would like to say thank you so much.

- Devin Jenkins
- Emily Washington
- Teresa Foster
- Travell Smith
- Natosha Glatz
- Chaznic Calhoun
- Tia Williams
- Carl Smith
- Jasmine Branford
- Mr. David
- Britt Williams

Table of Contents

Acknowledgments   3

Introduction   10

Chapter 1   12

The Minors Gold He Fights to be His Own   13

My Lost and Found   14

Holding On To Her   15

Bell's In My Head   16

The Love That She Can't See   17

The Love in One Night   18

In Love with a Girl/On a Trip Mostly Alone   19

The Love for This Girl, but the Mother Says No   20

The Love for Someone but yet was Never Together   21

Life of Love   22

My Happy Love   23

The Return of Long Lost Love   24

My Love   25

How Deep is Your Love   26

Chapter 2   **28**

A Stressed Relationship   29

Hard Relationship   30

Seeking for Help   31

Sad When We Are Away; Happy When We Are Together   32

She Told Me She Cried   33

Giving Up; Moving On   34

Life of a Mean Child about to Come Back Out.   35

I Cry   36

The Separation   37

A Smile to a Frown   38

Body Cold - Heart Frozen   39

A Sad Christmas   40

Chapter 3   **42**

My Eyes   43

My Wife   44

Why Am I A Lie to Her   45

Did I Make the Right Choice   46

How Can I   47

Why Can't She Make Up Her Mind   48

The Question I Have No Answer For   49

The Love for Someone but is it for an Angel or Demon?   50

The Questions of my Love   51

Why Love   52

The Question of True Love   53

Can I   54

Date   55

Should You   56

"WHY"   57

Chapter 4   **59**

We're Going To Make It   60

Making a Family   61

The Search   62

I Will Make It   63

A Climb to New Life   64

New Plan   65

New Life   66

Working My Way Up   67

The Maze   68

Past to Future   69

The Turn-Around   70

Time for a New Story   71

Chapter 5   **73**

Making Love to What's not Mine   74

Love Tackle   75

Passion   76

"Body Dancing"   77

"Little Secret"   78

"Swimming"   79

"Be Different"   80

Chapter 6   **82**

By Her Side   83

Bliss   84

A Chance for Her Heart   85

Life's A Game   86

The Girl of My Dreams But Yet Want To Be Friends   87

Feelings for her but we just Friends   88

A Chase that Seems Never Ending   89

My Favorite girl   90

One Time, One Chance   91

I see, I hear, I watch   92

The Glare in Her Eyes   93

This Christmas   94

Thinking of You   95

My Special Night   96

My Wonder   97

"The Turtle wins"   98

"He See Her"   100

"See Me, feel me"   101

"Runner"   102

"Gift"   103

"Glowing Feeling"   104

Too Much!!   105

Daydreaming   106

Perfect Match   107

"Was once mine"   108

"Let's get married"   109

" Everything"   110

"Mindtap"   111

Seeing Her Glow   112

"Never alone"   113

"King & Queen"   114

"Sipping Memories"   115

"The Rose"   116

"A Little Conversation"   117

"Have it all"   118

"Expiration date"   119

Chapter 7   **121**

What is your story   122

One True Love, but She Can't See   123

So Call Want To Be Wife   124

The Life I Went Through To Get My Love   125

The Happening   127

Stay My Angel   129

Life of Loving You   130

Watching   131

Reborn   132

Feeling Like You're Alone   134

Chapter 8   **137**

The Angel that Walks in Silence   138

My Angel   139

The Lord's Angel   140

Seeking for Help   141

Finally Got My Angel   142

Listen To the Word   143

I Died, but Through Her, I Live.   144

Conclusion   **146**

Introduction

It all started as a kid growing up in the streets of Miami.

Every summer, my mom would allow me to go and stay with my dad in Georgia. Even though I was supposed to be spending time with my dad, it wouldn't always end that way because he would have to work. He drove trucks for a living and would end up gone most days. During that time in Georgia for the summer, I would spend time with one of my cousins, and we would do everything together. One day my cousin decided to play this game of who could write the best poem. Since it was just the two of us, it would go like a rap battle. The first person to get the other one to *feel* what was being said would win.

We would laugh and go on like, "Yooo! Okay!" and "That's what's up. I like that; imma get you on the next one"; we loved it. Then when summer would end, I would go back to Miami with my mom. She knew at times I had a hard time expressing my feelings, so she gave me the idea to write them down in a book. She would say, "son, I know you like to be to yourself and hold on to your feelings and don't feel like talking about them, but instead of just holding on to them, get you a book and just write them down and express yourself that way and whatever you are feeling, release it in your book." So I did just that. And that is how this book came to be. I hope as you read, it shows you how to be comfortable doing the same. You may not be good with words, or it may be just hard for you to talk about how you feel.

But I encourage you to pick up a book and write it all down to release all that pent-up emotion in your writing. If what started out as a game could help me and allow me to have the courage to share it with the world, then I'm sure it can help you as well. Whether you keep it to yourself or one day, you too may want to share your writing with the world. Either way, you will feel better, and you will learn never to be afraid of your emotions; you will conquer them.

CHAPTER 1

Love

Love is something that comes with a lot of emotion. It can be painful or it can be happy, and it can be the best feeling ever but also the worst feeling, so when you take this journey into love, you will be able to open up those feelings and express those feelings that love made you feel.

The Minors Gold He Fights to be His Own

All through the day and all through the night, he mined for his gold. As he mined deeper into the cave, finding chips sparkling, but yet they weren't really worth anything. He took these little chips, dropped them into a black bag, and kept on moving. He traveled deeper day and night; day and night, searching for gold until one day, he struck something big. He dug and dug until finally, he came across a big beautiful piece of gold that could make him rich for the rest of his life. He pulled it out and all of a sudden, the cave began to shake. Bits and bits of the cave began to fall and then he noticed he was far back in the cave and that he had to run. So he ran. He ran, fighting his way through the cave, never letting go of the gold he found to be his own.

My Lost and Found

I lost her a year ago; I found her the following year.

She saw me; I saw her, I wanted her, and she wanted me. But the past was what kept her from taking me back. So I lost her again, but then I re-found her. Since that day, I was determined to get her heart back till I finally got it, and now I'm happy. She is the blood that keeps my heart pumping; she is the spirit running through my veins. I love her, and she loves me. She is my lost and found.

Holding On To Her

I see her; I see straight through her.

I can see that her heart has been broken. I'm here to be with her; I'm here to take care of her.

Give me your hand and hold on tight. Come along for the ride; I will not bite. I'm here to love you and put your heart on tight.

Bell's In My Head

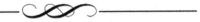

Bells ring in my head; they all chime different things.
Bell to the right says don't trust her; do your thing.
Bell to the left says trust her; have faith,
and y'all will make it.
Bell in the back says you are stupid; get it together.
Bell in the front says you're doing the right
thing; just have faith.
All these bells are making me crazy;
I'm losing my mind.
I'm crying for help. I love her; I need her.
I'm just going to put it up to the Lord
and let him lead the way.

The Love That She Can't See

I see her; she sees me.
My love for her is like her eyes are blind to see.
I struggle to clear them.
Hard to renew them; she can't see my love.
So it's like her eyes stay blind.

The Love in One Night

I saw her; she saw me.
We both glowed in each other's eyes.
She always saw me and I'd make her smile.
We finally started talking; then it was like
love in one night.
Our love grew bigger; we can see no other.
We only see each other; our hearts grow
within each other.

In Love with a Girl/On a Trip Mostly Alone

I was in love with a little girl and never knew what was coming. I wanted her to grow up and be a woman, but yet she stayed a youngin. She changed me, but I couldn't change her. She cheated and I stayed seated and went along for the ride. She took my heart, and now it's tart; I don't think I can go back and love her again. I planned to marry her, but she took the things that others said into belief and broke me. I cried; I tried, but in the end, it's like my heart says she wanted to be apart. I was in love with a little girl and tried to make her a woman. We never kissed; we never touched. So within the whole trip, I was mainly alone.

The Love for This Girl, but the Mother Says No

I love this girl, but her mother says no.
I treasure this girl, but her mother says no.
No matter what I try, her mother just keeps saying no.
I love this girl and she loves me back; we can't even be
around each other because her mother says no.
Her only reason is that she says that I'm too old.
We are still going to be together and fight through it
all, no matter how many times her mother says no.

The Love for Someone but yet was Never Together

In love with a beautiful brown angel but got betrayed by his own brother. He chased her for three years, then when things got clear, his brother came along and filled her head with lies and fear. He loved her so much that when he lost her, he cried, and all he did was stay in his room and hide. He loved the girl so much that even though they weren't together, she was the only one on his mind, and he tried his hardest to stay kind. Betrayed by his brother and was lost for almost forever. All he can do is think about the one he loved but was never together.

Life of Love

I feel as if I'm in competition for the girl of my dreams. She says she don't want a relationship, but yet this boy, that boy, boys around the way are always in her face and steadily sliding in my way. Love hurts; it really hurts when the one you truly love you can't have. Sometimes I find myself struggling trying to bring the light. This boy, that boy, I'm steadily juggling, but it seems the only effect I have is that I got them with height. Life of love is a very hard thing. I love this girl and the joy she brings.

My Happy Love

I saw her, and I began to like her off sight. So I spread my wings and took flight. I started vibin with her, and she reeled me in on the first bite. At first, I was scared, thinking she was going to eat me up and spit me out like a human crunching on a fish bone. She took me in and we got close. We became a couple and started vibin more. And we got so close that we made love for the first time in her home. We made love and were so happy. We were having so much fun, the next time we made love, it led to us starting a family. I love her and she says that she really loves me, and our next step into our love is preparing for this family.

The Return of Long Lost Love

My first love is back, and she is still as cute as a baby kitten. She found me on Facebookand at first, I just looked. We talked about our past, and now it's in a cast buried 6 feet under the ground. She asked for me back for the third time in her life, and as the question came out, my mind went blank. I told her I will trust her, and as I said it, my mind growled like an angry dog. I'm going with the flow, watching the grass grow, and as I fly, I'm looking for the beautiful green grass so my feet can finally leave the sky.

My Love

My love is pure. My love is strong. My love is real. Could you love me the same? Could you be here when I'm at my lowest and feel nothing is going right? Could you look at me every day forever? I could love you with everything in me and never second guess it, could you? I could love you forever till my dying days, but could you do the same? Could you still be here when I have my moments of just wanting to be to myself and relax my mind? For a long time, I pushed my feelings to the side, fearing to ever use them again. Could you be here to help me regain my trust in using them again? I could love you even at your worst moments, but could you love me at mine? Waking up alone is peaceful, but not better. Could you wake up every morning and see me and be truly happy? Not thinking about settling down because I've been so focused on being by myself. Could you give me what I've been missing, keeping me on my toes? When I go the wrong way, could you be here to turn me back around? My love is pure. My love is strong. My love is real. But could you?

How Deep is Your Love

How deep is your love? Is it deep enough that I can trust you with heart, and you give me your all? Is it deep enough to where we get in an argument, you either split the bed with pillows or make me sleep on the couch, but we find a way to fix it? How deep is your love? Is it deep enough that you will be my backbone and pick me up when I'm down? Is it deep enough to motivate me to never settle for less and always keep a positive mind? Is it deep enough where even through the bad, you stand right by me as my Queen? How deep is your love? Is it deep enough that we stand strong together with no worries? Is it deep enough that you are proud to be my woman and care less what others think or have to say, and I can be proud to be your man?

How deep is your love?

— 66 —

Permission for my brother to take the time to relax and calm your spirits and express the love that you feel.

— 99 —

CHAPTER 2

Pain

Pain is one of the worst feelings ever, but it's what makes us stronger. Walk through this journey and release that pain to understand you have not walked this journey alone.

A Stressed Relationship

I love her; she didn't see it.
I trusted her; she cheated.
I tried to get her to trust me, but she never
wanted to believe it.
I stressed out till I passed out. She took my heart and
dismantled it; I tried my best to handle it.
She has me so stressed out; my mind stays twisted out.

Hard Relationship

I found her; she found me.
I took her in; she followed me through.
I announced her; she announced me.
I thought we could make it till I found out
she was faking it.
I took her out; she tried to take me out, but my work is
so great I could never get put out.
I'm starting a new life; I'm moving on.
She can just take it because I'm going to make it.

Seeking for Help

My life is gone.
The devil comes out.
He takes my soul; I look down and frown.
I'm lost within the earth, nowhere to be found.
Lord, seek out my soul.
Bring me back to life.
Make me your angel and I shall be crowned.

Sad When We Are Away; Happy When We Are Together

I'm mad; I hear her voice, but there is no sound.
I miss her; I want to hold her. Give me her; I'll take
her. I love her; I'm going to marry her. When I'm not
with her, I'm down; I frown.
When I'm with her, I'm crowned; she is my
queen, I am her king.
When we are away, we can never shine.
When we are together, we are just fine.

She Told Me She Cried

That morning she said she cried the whole day. I tried
to believe her, but the way she's acting,
I think she lied.
I tried to make it work, but she can never see how hard
I try. She told me she had cried; that night,
I did the same.
I cried for her to see my love,
but the more I try, the more pain inside.
She told me she cried, but the way she lies, it's like a
person saying they can see through the sky.

Giving Up; Moving On

I feel that it's over; she has drifted away from me like a boat, slowly out to sea. I cared for her; I truly wanted to be with her, but she never took me in. This is the fourth year, and I haven't heard from her yet. She has gone loose like an escaped dog in heat and left her protection like a scared puppy. She left me alone, so I guess it's time for me to move on. I'm going to live my life and let her live hers. I'm not going to stop caring for her, but it's not going to be the same. My emotions for her are drifting away like the movie "Cast Away," and I'm coming back with a whole new appearance and keeping my feelings and emotions for her closed in and just don't care anymore and just rebirth myself like a newborn baby coming into this world.

Life of a Mean Child about to Come Back Out.

I've tried to stay clean. I've tried to stay in between, but these shones keep pushing it, and they are going to see a side they have never seen. People say I'm mean; even my mom says I'm mean. They are so blind they can't even see how I've been trying to stay clean. I walk around pissy then when they see it, they try to be all kissy. I've tried to be cool, but this may be the year that they see me act a fool. Lord, keep me together and keep me cool; keep me on the right path so I can stay in a good mood.

I Cry

I cry because I love her.
I cry because she loves me,
but we don't love the same.
I cry because when I look into her eyes,
I see what I want but can't have.
I cry because I try. I cry because apart
I miss her, but together I'm happy.
I cry and I feel like I can fly and feel the
wind beating against my eyes.
I cry because I want her to be mine.
I cry! I cry! I want her to be mine, and when I'm
around her, my heart begins to beat
like the rumbles of a drum.

The Separation

We came together; we vibed.
I found out about her and her past gave me hives.
She stayed in my life for a year,
so I tried to stay with her with no fear.
We fell in love, and our lives together began to grow,
but as it got closer for me to go,
her love began to stop like a river that lost its flow.
I started to get ready and she went from brave to scary.
So she asked to separate and I agreed and I expanded
my wings and took flight.

A Smile to a Frown

I smiled because I was happy, but bad things began to happen, and that smile left me.
I smiled because I was happy yet the one I was in love with is what gave me my frown.
She told me she loved me. She told me she wanted a family, but as soon as things got rough, she took off on me like a jet. It happened so fast; it was like watching Martin on Bad Boys jump from a big rat.
Now she is gone, and my smile is now a frown, but hey, I'll never let it put me down. I'm going to keep flying until my feet can touch a better ground.

Body Cold - Heart Frozen

Everyday I spend my days thinking of her, but for some reason I'm always sad. When I'm with her, I'm just as happy as I want to be, but away from her, I always get a negative vibe, and my body shuts down. It's like my body becomes really cold and my heart freezes. I find myself giving her all of me and not holding anything back. I asked her for her all and I got it but she still holds some back. I've done and said everything I could to get her to understand how much I love her and don't want to lose her. It's like I've lost my temperature, and I ask myself, where have my sunny days gone? Is there anywhere to stay warm? It's not easy when she's gone. Then I ask myself, how am I supposed to go on? So then I start to cry because I love her so much and some days I feel alone. I try to express myself and tell her how much I love her and she tells me she really loves me too, but I know she still holds back from me. My body is cold and my heart is frozen. God, please let her really and truly feel and take in all of my love and give me all of hers without holding back and wipe away my tears.

A Sad Christmas

Just when I thought my Christmas was going to be great, it turned out to be the worst. I did all I could and showed all the love she could ever have, yet the one I truly loved broke my heart. I expected to be with her, but she blocked me out and saw others. All night I tossed and turned, hurting and crying because I love her so much, and for her to do what she did to me hurt me deep down because my love for her is so strong. With everybody telling me to leave her and that she isn't any good; it's just not that easy. I'm fighting for her love. I'll do anything. Every time I think we are good, somehow she breaks me again, and I'm still hurting. I want to stop crying, stop hurting, and be happy. I want a real relationship.

— 66 —

Permission: My brother, I give you the permission to take the time out to relax, calm your soul, and release the pain you feel or have felt.

— 99 —

CHAPTER 3

Questions

Your emotions can leave you with a lot of questions and sometimes it's hard to express them. So as you take the trip down this journey of questions you too can feel comfortable to ask yourself those questions as well as feel free to write them down and get the answers you need.

My Eyes

My eyes, my eyes; please tell me I'm not blind.
I see her; she shines. I touch her; I unwind, but when I
hear her say things I don't want to hear;
my eyes begin to cry.
As she comes up to me it's like
I didn't hear anything so my eyes began to dry.
I love her; I care for her. My eyes, my eyes; please
show me I'm not blind.

My Wife

My wife, my wife; does she really want to be my wife?
I really love her; I really want her to be my life.
She tells me she does, but around people I'm not even
there. She looks at me as if she cares,
but showing it's just hardly there.
I'm happy, I'm sad; I want her to be my wife, but does
she really feel the same? Lord, please show me if she
feels the same.

Why Am I A Lie to Her

I love her; I tried to show her.
Every time I try to tell her she looks the other way.
I try the truth but to her it's all a lie.
I cry, but to her I lie.
I'm just going to look towards the sky; only God
knows I won't lie.
Lord, dry my eyes, and my soul shall not die.

Did I Make the Right Choice

Struck by surprise; mind can't believe its eyes. Waking up to a blank number; texting back to find out this blank someone is my ex, my old love, my first love. Jumping out of nowhere, she comes back to me; with me finding out she wants me back.

Her other love left her to the basics. So she turned to me and I started casin. She told me she was sorry. She says she wants me back, but in the back of my mind saying you don't need the stress, but the other half saying do what's best. I cased it and I got my answers. I took her back; now the last thing to do is to just sit back and see what's next and see if the choice I made was the best.

How Can I

How can I gain her trust?
How can I gain her heart?
How can I show her how much I care?
I've been hurt for a long time and
I know that she has too.
I'm ready to settle and ready for her. She says she is
not ready, like she's full of fear and all I want to do is
show her that I'm here.
How can I show her I'm here when others are always
near and her heart is full of fear?

Why Can't She Make Up Her Mind

We talk every now and then.

I like her but she doesn't like me.

When another female gets involved, she gets hot like a
mother that has to pay a high fee. I think to myself,
why me? Why can't she just make up her mind?

So I can really know if she wants to be with me. I'm
sitting in ISS and in my 4th block class I have a test.

I'm just sitting here thinking about her trying
to figure out what's best.

The Question I Have No Answer For

The day has come and the question is starting to flow.
From morning to noon the question begins to grow. I
have no answer for but people began to show.

They all ask the same question and now I'm full
of passion. I'm stuck with a question that
I have no answer to.

I'm hoping it will come like my mom
praying for a new home.

I'm gradually falling for her but can't complete the
question. I'm stuck with a question; a question
with no answer.

The Love for Someone but is it for an Angel or Demon?

I took flight from old love and landed on new.

I found this one, and she stood out like a beautiful angel, and we fell in love, but sometimes the way she acts, it's like I just fell in love with a beautiful demon.

She wants to start a family, but she holds so much from me I don't think she can handle me or the love I bring.

Angel or Demon I'm praying for angel because if she's a demon playing with my heart, then my body shall perish and fall apart.

The Questions of my Love

Why must I love so strong?
Why must I love so deep?
Why must I love at all?
My questions are hard to answer because I find
myself falling in love with an angel that
I'm not sure really loves me back.
I'm staying with her because every time I speak or am
around her, my heart goes racing like a NASCAR flap.
All I know is that she tells me she loves me and she
wants to start a family. With me.
So I'm going to take this chance and play my cards
right and keep my eyes open and pay attention to
everything like a pirate on the open sea.

Why Love

The way some people love you can't help but ask why?

Because love has this strong hold that when it hurts, you cry. You can find yourself telling a person your deepest feelings for them, but they will never tell you theirs. But then you find out the reason why is because the same stuff you're saying to them, they are saying to somebody else.

And that's when your love truly hurts. Once that happens, you find yourself asking, why love?

The Question of True Love

Stumbling and fumbling asking myself what is love? Is it the time you are happy and everything's going right? Or it's the time you are hurting, crying, and fighting to make somebody else happy for their love. So, again I ask, what is love? What is true love? I'm stuck between the two, steadily asking this question because I feel like I'm fighting for love but don't really know if she truly loves me back or just telling me what I want to hear. So, I ask again, what is love? What is true love? Is it that feeling you get when you get around that person and your heart pumps harder, but you're at a loss of breath and no words come out? Or is it when you are around that person, and you feel happy? Like you can tell them any and everything, and yall both get along with no fussing or anything. Just pure happiness. Or is it when you're mad at each other and always fussing and having problems? Now I ask for a final time, what is love? What is true love?

Can I

Can I love you until the day God calls us home? Can I
hold you through the nights keeping you warm and
safe? Can I wake up and give you a good morning kiss
to your forehead; to your soft warm lips?

Can I lay into your eyes and you lay into mine and we
see into our souls; seeing the pain that was to the love
that's being shown? Can I express my love to you
without seeming soft or less than a man and I sit and
listen to your love for me?

Can I make deep love to you, looking into each other's
eyes, holding each other close, full of passion? Can I
hold you down where I got your back and you got my
front and we stand side by side together strong? Can
we make each other smile, knowing we got each other
and nothing can come in between? You are a queen,
you are beautiful, you are amazing, and I just want to
know, can I?

Date

Hey, can I get a minute of your time? Tell you how beautiful I think you are from my point of view. Can we exchange numbers and keep in contact with each other? If you allow me to, I would like to take you on a date. Not like how they are doing now with Netflix and chill, but an actual dinner and movie and explore something that's real. Sit down and talk and get to know each other. Explain our wants and needs. I'm trying to pick your mind; make you smile and giggle. Feel the energy between each other through conversation giving each other butterflies inside making our bodies tickle. We don't have to get physical. At this moment I'm exploring your mental. All I'm asking is for a little bit of your time. Sit down and let's talk; I got you. Think about it and if you say yes then let the motion picture begin and make this movie exploring each other's minds and see where time takes us.

Should You

Body tired, mind is numb, heart is crying.

Why when you're supposed to be happy, yet it feels so painful? Like you're fighting in a battle like a Spartan without his 300. You're all alone; no help, it's just you, and in the mist, you pause, and something hits you, and you stare off into space, wondering, is this fair? You thought you had a partner, but it starts to look as if your partner is against you and stopped fighting. Body gets tired, mind goes numb, heart begins to hurt. Then you find yourself in the midst of the battle asking yourself if you should keep fighting. Body tired, mind numb, heart crying, stomach trembling, not knowing if the fight should go on. So you ask yourself, "should you?"

"WHY"

Questioning myself. Why does everything about you feel amazing to me? From the rays of your beautiful smile. Seeing you smile brightens up my day like the beautiful sunrise each morning. The giggle of your laugh when I say something stupid, even tho it may not be that funny, it seems to still give you a tickle. Talking to each other in an intellectual and spiritual mindset. We connect like puzzle pieces but push each other away at times. Like trying to put the wrong sides of a magnet together, fearing getting hurt. Like two songbirds that broke their wings and are scared to fly again. How I love your independence not needing a man. You're not afraid to do things on your own. It turns me on, wanting you even more, and my vibe you can't resist, like your favorite song you can't help but vibe to every time you hear it. Why do I feel this way about you? Why do you feel this way about me? Everything feels so perfect; your touch sends chills down my body like the brisk wind in the moonlight. Just seeing your face and making you smile makes everything feel just right. Feeling speechless at times, all I do is sit back and just ask, "Why?"

——————— 66 ———————

*Permission: now that you have made it through,
now take your time to relax and calm your soul
and express the questions you also have.*

——————— 99 ———————

CHAPTER 4

Striving feelings

We all strive to be better or feel better or have a better relationship; whatever it is, we strive for better. So feel free to walk this journey and express what you strive to feel better in.

We're Going To Make It

I spotted her; she spotted me.
We clicked at first sight; we matched at first bite.
We fell for each other; we took each other in.
Rocks fell in our path, but nothing is
coming in our way.
We are fighting through it all; we are going to take it.
We are going to be together, and there is nobody or
nothing out there that can break it.

Making a Family

She has a son; I have myself.
Put us together then there will be a family.
She takes care of me and him; I take care of them.
We can be a family; we just have to make it.
We may have hard times, but that's what families do.
We can make it; we just have to handle it.
We are a family, and we will make it.

The Search

I went through a bad past. Now I'm roaming through the future on a big search and left my past in a cast. I'm searching for her; I'm searching for the one. I'm on a mission looking for that special woman. I'm going to treat her right. Send me that angel that I can keep and it will be right. I'm on this search trying to find her and praying it will be a better life.

I Will Make It

I watched people live happily. I watched people live through crises, but in my world, that's just the way of life. I've grown from a little boy through the life of Miami to a hard life as a teen in little Miami. I grew up on sports but never that good on the court, but put me on some pads and let me touch the field, and boy, I'm a tough quick shield. Take me off the field and put me on the track, and boy, I'm telling you, I can scat. I'm a great person to be with, but getting on my bad side can be the hardest to deal with. I'm trying to make it through safely, so I'll just have faith and I will make it.

A Climb to New Life

Burning in hell; I can't take the smell.

I roam around searching for the light. I spotted the
small hole, but yet somehow it's so bright.

I'm climbing to the top, trying to make it to the light.
Small and big objects are trying to take my might, but
I'm going to keep climbing through, praying until I
make it through to the light.

New Plan

New ground has been gained. New choices
have been made.

Now working to my goals and going down a different
path waiting for the right one and still moving on.

Life has changed for me and a lot has gone on, but I'm
not going to let it keep me down. I'm on a different
side of the mountain with new holsters on a better
climb with no plans on falling again.

New Life

Okay I went through pain and wrote it and now my heart has gone through a complete change. Gaining my love will be a hard thing. Having strong feelings will take awhile. So my heart is closed until I really find the right one. No more stressing, no more being love struck, and no more feelings going in deep. Now it's a new story in my life. A new phase of travel to manage and work toward my goals and wait for love and just keep my eyes open.

Working My Way Up

I tried so hard and came so far. At one point I was stuck at the bottom and now I'm making the movement to the top.

It's hard; this climb I'm on, but I'm slowly making it and gradually climbing for a higher note. I'm working my way up, reaching for greatness.

Let me end this on a high note. I'm working my way up, seeking for the best.

The Maze

The glow of her smile, the cheer in her laugh, the softness of her body, the calmness she has around me. Through all of that I can look into her eyes and feel that she has been hurt.

I know this feeling because I, too, have been hurt. But bringing me down will not work. Struck by her smile I know I'm in for a round, but I'm going to keep on going because I'm never backing down. She's able to trust me; we are off to a good start. I'm in a maze to her heart and once I get it I'm holding on to it and never letting it fall apart.

Past to Future

Mind clear, body warm, but my heart is like icy hot.
Hot on the outside keeping my blood warm and
pumping steady, but cold on the inside freezing and
locking away all the pain it's ever been through.

I remember my pain but only for the best;
to build my future and forget the rest.

I've been through a lot and trying to stand strong but
sometimes my past just won't leave me alone. So I'm
just going to keep pushing my way through, making
my future right, walking with an icy hot heart,
keeping the bad out of my sight.

The Turn-Around

I went through hard crises; now I'm out and life has been very bright. I cried about the past; now I'm moving happily through the future. I made a big turn around because in the past I just couldn't stand it. Now I'm making this big turn so that I can take the future and live on. I've made this big turn in life but I couldn't have made it without the help of Jesus Christ.

Time for a New Story

I write this book to express my feelings, but going through them I feel that they're all the same. All I talk about is love and the way I feel and they all talk about some girl that's been hurt or hurting me.

I need a new story. I need a new life. I need something new and it needs to be right; so it's time to begin a whole new life.

Permission: my brother, you have made it through another one. Now take the time to relax and calm your soul and express where you are striving to next in your journey of emotions.

CHAPTER 5

Sexual

Sex is such a wonderful feeling but it also can make us make the wrong decisions. Sometimes we engage in it just to fill that desire, but constantly sharing that desire with multiple people will never fill it. Sharing that with one person truly worth sharing that desire with makes it the best feeling ever and downright amazing. So walk this journey into sex and share that desire with your partner and make it not just a feeling to fill a desire but make it amazing with that one person that allows you to express your sexual desires.

Making Love to What's not Mine

I met this angel that walked in silence like a beautiful white bengal. She came down to me with this bright glow. I finally got her, and boy I tell you we put on a show. I fell in love with her; she fell in love with me, but this demon came out of nowhere and her love left me and grew stronger for him. I fell from her for a moment but she always came back to me because when we make love, it's the best ever. Yet still she finds herself with him. I find myself in love with someone that love is not as strong as mine for me. Leaving me thinking that I'm making love to what's not mine. Asking myself why am I so kind, but I can't answer it because I want her to be mine; I'm just waiting for my chance to have all of her love, but until then I'm just making love to what's not mine.

Love Tackle

It all starts when we walk into the room.

I lay you down and give you a kiss that sends a warm
climax feeling through your body letting you
know it's about to go down.

From the kiss of your lips, down to your breast, down
biting into your hips, down between your legs with a
motion you can't and don't want to escape, and your
body can't fight but enjoys the pleasure I'm bringing as
I go in deeper.

You can't help but feel so right. As I put it down you
can't help but hold me tight.

Passion

The hunger for something that you want so bad you will do whatever for it. Even when no one believes you should have it. Something you will sacrifice whatever you have to in order to get there. That one thing you know and believe you should have, and you're gunning for it.

"Body Dancing"

When you are around me I just lose all control. I can't help myself around you. I can't help but see your glow. I just want the glow you light up in me to intertwine with yours and everything just flows. When you're not around me I see your image dancing on my body. The image of you walking through the room. I'm just watching your body flow and it's so smooth and just right my rode began to grow. I lose all control because you have woken every zone in my body and all my mind is saying is it's on. I got to have you so as I lay you down I began to play with every inch of your body and every motion I made your body dances. Tongue begins to play in your pie with twists and turns that causes you to malfunction in every direction but holding me in place so I stay right in that spot. Realizing this is just the beginning. You would have thought it was a plot but you enjoy it so much you don't want it to stop. Covered in your juices it's now time for my rode to erupt and as he enters your body pores as you take that gasp for air as I take my time to drive through.

In every stroke, she gets wetter. In every stroke, she grips tighter. In every stroke, the more she loses control till we both are dancing in motion with no control. Filled with so much bliss and warmth and excitement that we have officially lost control and in a blissful role.

"Little Secret"

Look into his eyes and see that you're safe. Lay your head across his chest and let him hold you and feel that you are in the right place. Let him caress your body as he helps you relax. He is here to release your stress. So while he is here, give him your best. Y'all are each other's secret, and he is going to put your body to the test, from the kisses of your lips to massaging your body along the way. Tickling your neck with his tongue while pulling down your thong. Relax your body and give him all of you because the beginning of the pleasures had just begun. Massaging your breast while twirling his tongue around your nipples. Gripping your hips while working down your stomach. Kissing your hips, biting into your pelvis. Lifting your legs up high, kissing, biting, and sucking down your thighs. Working his way to the middle as he puts your lips into his mouth and his tongue licking on your clit. Tongue dancing in and out your wet warm hole while sucking on your lips, tasting all your wetness that you explode. Hands massaging your butt while he works out your love below. Then slowly works his way up to inject his warm hard pipe into your warm wet hole. He pulls you close and you hold him tight as he slides in and out, filling you cover him with all your wet waters. Y'all are each other's secret relieving each other of the stresses through the bodies of each other till the end, where nothing is left but sleeping in peace.

"Swimming"

Look into my eyes while I kiss those lips as I prepare to take a swim with passion. I'm diving in deep; ocean. I got you in position; focus. Tell me what you want while I'm strokin, find your hand placement. Imma give you what you want; while you hold me closer. Switching up speeds got you fallin for the kid. Switch up the position and grab a handful of hair, make that back arch. Grip that neck while watching that ass wave. This passion is going to have you feeling a way; when you look at me, that body will shake.

"Be Different"

Let's do something different; nobody has to
know about us.

Distance doesn't matter because the pull up
will be worth every moment.

We can just be ghosts to the world, just me and you.
Let me fill your cup and drink you up. You will get all
my time; trust me I'm able. Let me tamper with your
mind for a minute. You don't have to say much
because in a minute we are about to make some good
love. Watch me spread your legs and get ready for
some rounds tonight.

Filling each appetite making you cream from every
stroke. Making love, feeling each other vibe; making
me cuss as I'm making you bust.

Enjoying the moment reaching each other's peak when
it's all over lay your head on my chest and hold each
other through the rest of the night.

> *Permission: now that you have reached the end, calm your mind and relax your soul and express your sexual desires.*

CHAPTER 6

Bliss

The journey into bliss is a walk where you have times when things just happen in the moment. You can be just living your life and a moment happens unexpectedly. Sometimes it can leave you feeling confused or just wondering why. So express those moments and feel free to write them down. Release and let go.

By Her Side

I see her sad; she's always mad, but what keeps her
going is knowing I'm by her side.

I love her; I care for her, but to see her hurting
I can't bear to stare.

I watch her get up; feels broken down and hurt,
feeling there is no hope inside,

but as long as she knows I'm by her side; she doesn't
have to worry about the whole day being sad.

Bliss

The moment I saw her everything in me lit up like a light. Telling myself I had to have her, I was determined to get her with all my might. Connecting with her through cybor connection my determination was put in motion. Everything flowed like a steady ocean. I was getting everything I needed so when the time came I knew just how to flow. The time came for us to finally meet and everything in me went rushing full of excitement like a kid hyped on sugar. Nervous but happy at the same time. I spoke it into existence that I had to have her and it's finally happening. It's earlier than I expected but it's happening. Meeting for drinks everything went as I planned and it blew like a calm steady night. We laughed and enjoyed the moment of being in each other's presence. It's getting late so we head back to the room and from there it was all bliss. So blissful it was like fireworks on the 4th of July. We exploded all through the night. The night ended perfectly; so much so, we didn't want to leave each other. But we knew if I stayed what would have happened. So we ended the night but left each other with so much joy that everytime we speak to each other we smile. So bright that even the sun can't compete. Now we count down the days to our next embrace.

A Chance for Her Heart

I feel her; she feels me.

I like her; she likes me, but her feelings
you can't believe.

She's been hurt more than a year now; she's full of
fear like a rabbit running from a wolf.

I'm here to un-break it; hoping she will take it. I'm just
letting her know if she just gives me her heart; I
promise not to break it.

Life's A Game

Games are played; new systems are made.

Find the right game and the sticks won't get put down.

Find the wrong game; then the headaches
will be found.

Life is a game; people fight for the best ones.

If you get stuck with the wrong one don't
make headaches, just keep fighting through it
and you will make it.

The Girl of My Dreams But Yet Want To Be Friends

The girl of my dreams!

Through the nights I dream of her. Through classes I sleep; she's always on my mind. She never has to stay behind nor stand in line; she can just walk on up and take her crown and stand right by my side.

She is the queen of my world and the angel of my soul. I really want to be with her and nothing's going to stop me. I will have her in my arms holding her tight.

Feelings for her but we just Friends

I love to see her happy. Through her down and outs just seeing my face and being around me makes her happy.

She has a smile as bright as the sun; she glows in my eyes like the brightest star twinkling through the night.

She is my walking angel and being around her and talking to her lifts my spirits. She runs through my mind like beautiful white rabbits running through the wild.

We are friends now but one day she will hopefully be my queen. And when that day comes we shall be the happiest couple ever.

A Chase that Seems Never Ending

I talked to her for the first time and I loved the way she spoke and acted.

I saw her for the first time and from then my eyes opened and my chase had begun. She stepped into my life and my world began to change. She went through a bad relationship the first year and I cleared her way through. We grew closer and we became best friends to where we could tell each other anything and everything. She began to feel me as more than just a friend yet she would never be with me. I tried and I tried but I just kept getting denial after denial. She kept telling me she really likes me. Years run by and it's about to be the fourth year and she is still not in my arms and I really want her to be. It's like a never ending chase that I just can't complete and I really want my chocolate bunny all to myself. She is my never ending chase.

My Favorite girl

She is my favorite girl. Give me the chance
and I'll be her favorite man.

She glows in my eyes; she is like a beautiful
bird flying through the skies. I want to give her
the world; I'm just waiting for her to come down
and touch the floor.

She is my favorite girl; she is the one I want in my
world. Give me a chance. I know she'll love to be a
part of it. Take my hand and let's fly away. She will be
safe with me in a happy world.

She is my favorite girl.

One Time, One Chance

One time, one chance
Break your heart; I just can't.
I look at you and you seem to be happy, but the
glow in your eyes seems to be fading.
One time, one chance and I will fight to keep you
happy. Trust in me, believe in me and I promise
to be the one for you.
I'm not out to hurt you, only want to help
you and make you happy.
One time, one chance and I promise to
take care of you.

I see, I hear, I watch

I see a lot, I hear a lot, and I watch everything. But in the end is it all worth it?

Every day it's a new look. Every day it's a new hearing. I sit back a lot and just watch it all. Some things I see, but most of it I just hear. It makes me mad with some of the stuff I hear, but I just keep it moving. I see a lot of things, but things you see are different from what you watch. What you see is just a glimpse that catches your eyes then it's gone, but the things you watch are something that catch your eyes, and you can't take your eyes off of. I see a lot, but I'm watching one thing and hoping for the best. So, for now, all I can say is, "I see, I hear, I watch."

The Glare in Her Eyes

I looked into her eyes and just looked.

All I could see was somebody I wish I could be with.
I slept into her eyes trying to see more and
my body went into stealth.

I went in for a kiss and all I got was a miss.
We had our talk and she said she doesn't want a
relationship, but when I looked into her eyes,
I saw something different.

Maybe it's just my eyes; I don't know, give me another
sign. The glare in her eyes tell me one thing, but her
actions speak a whole nother language and I'm lost
trying to fight through both of them.

This Christmas

This Christmas is special because not only is it the day baby Jesus was born, but it's the day I have my true love. So I took her hand and we flew away like two beautiful doves. This Christmas is special because it's full of love. The love for your family, the love of a husband and his wife and kids. This Christmas is special because I have my love, and she has me, and this year, not only do I get to say "Merry Christmas," I also get to tell my true love, "I love you."

Thinking of You

I think of you the most when I'm feeling happy or sad or any other emotions. When I think of you I get this tingling feeling inside of me. I love the way you smile because to me it seems that you're making everything right and completing my day. When I hear your voice I'm sure that you won't do anything to ever hurt me. When you walk past me I just stare at you because of your beauty, and at times I think that I fall too deep for you and then one day may come that you crush my heart. I pray all the time that you don't because I love you with everything in me.

My Special Night

She stayed for the first night and for me it was wonderful. The joy of her smile, the embrace of her body. She made my night special; she was my star of the night.

Laying here waiting for her next embrace she did so much that my mind wandered into thinking about just having the shine of her smile, and the laughs through the night till we laid down to sleep. She was my star of the night, my wonder of the night. She is so special to me, I'm just laying here waiting for her next embrace.

My Wonder

When I first saw you, you glowed in my eyes. Your beautiful smile shined like the sun in the sky. I wanted to get to know you, and I got to hold you. Out of respect for you and your body, I just enjoyed the embrace and tried to hold you tight so you would feel safe. Life went on as we passed a few words. My mind still wanders how it would have been to commit myself to you, but the words "I don't want you" are stuck in my head like glue. I lay back and think, what did I do wrong? Did I come on too strong? But I was never in a rush because jumping into a relationship wasn't a must. So as life goes on, sometimes I miss you and wish I could kiss you because of the beauty of your smile; I can't lie; the curves of your hips expand my eyes. I saw the out, hoping to get to know the in. Being around you made me happy, like a child getting their favorite teddy bear.

"The Turtle wins"

You thought you were hot every since you started poppin. Men all in ya DM and running up to you when they see you and telling you how sexy you are and how you killin ya outfits. 100 plus likes on social media got you feeling like you on top of the world. Man comes along to speak to you and tell you how beautiful you are and look at you as a Queen and not just some piece of meat. You pass him along because you consider him a lame because he is trying to tap into your mind frame and see what you want to be in life and not trying to hurry up and lay down on a bed frame. While you pass him along bc you consider him to be a lame you jump up and give these little boys a chance bc they buy you nice things partying with you. Dopping you up and you now you done fucked around and gave him your heart and he don't even feel the same. So now your little heart broken don't know what to do; feeling stupid inside bc you made another wrong choice. Then another man comes along and you pass him along too. All because you're hurting about the choice you made. Went to playing around with them fuck boys now ya lil heart ain't the same. Now you running around saying fuck a nigga. The only thing on your mind is running up a check. Out partying and doing ya thing until you go back to that empty house lonely saying dang I wish I had someone to cuddle and talk with bc this lonely shot is not a fun game. Ha!! You was hot, alright; hot enough to fuck but not hot enough to wife. Then you run into or see that man that you considered to be a lame, and now he is doing to one Queen what he wanted to do with you, and all you can say is, damn, that could have been me if you would have actually given him a chance. Ha!! And that's the price you pay when choosing a fuck boy over a man...

"He See Her"

I see you and your glow dances in my eyes like the fire burning on the end of a candle stick. Your smile is so bright it's like it's my morning sunshine every morning I can't wait to see it. When you're down it's like a night with a half moon and I just want to be your sun to lift you back up. Your silliness tickles me. I can't help but enjoy you. If I'm taking too much of your time let me know and I'll let you go. If not can I take you out and get to know the inner you to see if your inner self is just as wonderful as your glow on the outside. I know when you laid out your story you didn't see me in it because I didn't see you in mine. But I'm not trying to change it, I just want to add to it to see if we write our story like a Harry Potter. Or will it end shortly like a simple-by-day book like a Dr. Seuss book? My goal is to combine both my story alone with yours and we go beyond a Harry Potter book but a story of me and you. Through ups and downs, happiness and joy, sunny and stormy days. Your presence makes my day, and to have you in it, if possible, I hope I can make yours too, and we make each other's day. If yes, let our story begin, and we will continue to write together.

"See Me, feel me"

Close your eyes. Relax your mind. Follow my voice. Understand everything I'm saying and feel just how real I am as I run my hand across your cheeks feeling your beauty. Envision everything I'm telling you and let it touch your soul till everything in you feels safe. Then allow me to wrap my arms around you and just hold you tight as our warm body's relax on each other. Allowing yourself to trust me becoming your King and you become my Queen. Placing my hands over your heart indicating that your heart is safe in my hands and I promise to take good care of it. In this moment we share together is a moment of us bringing our spirits together trusting together we are safe. Your inner beauty is just as important to me as what's on the outside; you continue to glow and your outer beauty shines like the brightest star. You trust me and I trust you. That is all I'm asking for in this moment.

We can grow and build from there. Once you have felt everything I've said to express what I'm after and you feel me deep down into your soul then open your eyes

"Runner"

The times we have spent together replay in my head like a skipping disk. Now the more time we spend apart, those moments slowly disappear, fading into the mist. Like a runner coming in last place wondering if he would ever get to first. Running at a steady pace while others continue to stay ahead or skip ahead in the race.

"Gift"

The moment they met, they lit up like fireworks. Never a dull moment with the two. Their bond grew closer; their love grew stronger. Committed to each other, they have been nothing but happy. Her warm kisses like the morning sun, and he loves every time they are in brace. Laying in his arms, she knows she is safe. Holding each other, they are at peace. Her smile shines so bright, like the stars through the night. Her laugh tickles him; he can't help but laugh with her. No gift, no special moment can ever make her feel as happy as he makes her because he is her gift, and she is his gift, so every moment together is their gift. No matter how down one can be, just talking to each other makes things better, and nothing else matters; no pain, no aggravation, no nothing can come between the two; there is each other happiness. Their love for each other is bigger than any problems they could ever have going on, and they battle through it together, standing side by side. She is his Queen, and he is her King.

"Glowing Feeling"

From the moment we met she moved something in me I didn't even think was still there. The first time I held her I felt peace. When I look into her eyes, I see all of her beauty. I want to get to know more about her, touch her, taste her; be the man in her life, and in her bed. Wanting to wake up beside her whenever I can; I want to be good to her. Have movie nights, dinner dates, walks in the park, just have fun and laugh together, enjoy each other. Isn't that what lovers do these days? That glow in her eyes every time she looks at me and puts on that beautiful bright smile moves me every time like the calmest wave on a beachfront and the sun shining straight through and hits the bottom. She is amazing and she makes me feel amazing. Her persona glows so perfectly that no matter where I'm at, she is right there in my mind, and I see her beauty and that beautiful smile, and I just smile with happiness and peace, and even when I'm away, she is everywhere I want to be.

Too Much!!

As you lay on my chest, I hold you. I feel like
it's everywhere I want to be.

Wanting to be able to feel free and express
my emotions to you; is it too much?

I feel as if an eternity with you isn't enough; is it too
much? A day without you feels like months to years of
emptiness; is it too much? When we make love to each
other, feel me dance inside with a sense of pride and
joy like yes, this is all mine; is it too much? When you
look at me, see me as me and accept me as me and
give me all your love, and in return, I give all of mine;
is it too much? Looking into your eyes is like the
whole world stops, and it's just us; is it too much?
Don't want to fall asleep. I rather fall in love; is it too
much? Can we take a walk on the beach but your first
steps, you jump into my arms because the touch of the
sand is too hot for your comfort and we laugh and the
sound of your laugh tickles my soul; is it too much?
Feeling free with you, I can't help but thank God for
what He has brought me; is it too much? When I'm
with you, I feel like I'm right where I'm supposed to
be; is it too much?

Daydreaming

As I lay here, I find myself daydreaming of her beauty and how amazing it is that my best friend is my girl. We combined our energy, and she allowed me to give what her past couldn't provide and every time she looks at me, it's like she is walking down the aisle to her King. She is the Nala to my Simba and our hearts flow together in perfect harmony. A blessing walking and every night I climax her to sleep, she sleeps in peace, knowing she has everything she has ever wanted. Laying in my arms, feeling safe and loved, she is perfect, and every moment I think of her, I can't help but smile.

Perfect Match

You are everything I could have imagined.
I see your face when I lay down.
I see you when I walk around the house.
I hear your voice and your laughter when
everything goes silent.
I see your smile when I close my eyes.
You are my perfect match.
The fun we have brings out our inner
child and it feels awesome.
Holding you feels so right nothing else matters.
Being in your presence makes even the worst
days feel like my best days.
Your motivation makes me stronger
and go even harder.
My fairy take love. I can never have eyes
for anyone else but you.
You are my perfect match.

"Was once mine"

Can't believe you gave him what was once mine. Making me feel like I was the best thing to ever happen to you. Who knew you were the devil's playground? Saint in the presence of my eyes, devil's angel when my back turned, feeding on every man that attracted you like a vampire out on a feeding frenzy. Finding out about your life outside of mine and you acted as if it was my fault. The devil having so much of a hold on you when I left in the moment, you felt free to do whatever without a care and without hiding until you got tired and realized it wasn't what you wanted and that I was the best you ever had and now your life is difficult trying to find what I once gave you and it's like damn, can't believe you gave away what was once mine.

"Let's get married"

Here we are, settled down. Every time I look at you, I'm like, sheesh, that's all me. All this time, we have put in with each other through the good and the bad.

We stood strong together. I can't help but say, let's get married. Love me long till the end; we have come a long way from single-town, and I know God will continue to see us through, and I will always stay 10 toes down. So let's get married. Watching you come down to the altar, my eyes glued to you like it was my first time seeing you in a crowd full of people but only having eyes for you. Nothing can really explain exactly how I feel other than we are unafraid of what the world has to say about us. And I know you feel it too. Here I am, just a man in love with a woman that I never want to let go, so let's get married as we continue to move forward in life together because, in this life of ours, I can't see myself with anyone but you. So I say let's get married.

" *Everything*"

Everything about you sits so perfect. Not being able to see you or hear your voice is like a prisoner stuck in solitary screaming but the only voice he hears is his own. Then the moment you appear is like the sun popping out after a stormy day and everything shines brighter off the flickers of the sun's rays. You are his smile, his joy, what makes him shine even when he doesn't feel he is. You are what makes him love to be him because he knows with you he has everything when he feels he has nothing. You are his strength when he feels weak; the star in his movie. You are EVERYTHING....

"Mindtap"

I see you and trust it's in the purest sight. I've noticed you because you walk in a different light. Sex is easy; that's light work. Now tapping into your mind; that's a different type of work. Taking time, patience, listening, understanding, trusting, focusing, and believing. Allowing you to paint me the picture of your dreams and goals so there is no one leader but a guidance together like Cloak and Dagger. Even when not around, we are still together. So as you allow me to understand; together we'll work out a plan.

Seeing Her Glow

The glow around her shines so bright, but on the inside is so gloomy it feels as if it wants to shut down, but her will to be strong is what keeps her going. He saw her, and her glow almost blinded him like a fool that stares at the sun. He approached her, and they exchanged words leaving her with a smile, but he could tell something was wrong, like walking into the woods and you get that feeling something isn't right. They later went out to eat, and instead of him spending his time telling her about him, he kept it short just so he could listen to her and find out what was wrong. He could tell something was off. In the end, he took her back to his place, and they talked more and he just held her. In his arms, she felt safe. In his arms, she relaxed as if she was on a beach soaking up the sun and feeling the breeze, listening to the ocean waves. Closed her eyes and dosed off because he made her feel as if everything was going to be alright. He looks at her, kisses her on the head, holds her tight, and closes his eyes to sleep. When they wake the next morning, she looks at him and smiles as if that's just what she needed, and she no longer felt so gloomy. She now glows inside and out, and being with him, she knew everything was going to be alright.

"Never alone"

His journey is beginning and even though he isn't alone, he can't help but feel alone. Every time he has gotten ready to step into his journey, he stops and prays and asks God to keep him strong. Every time he has stepped out, he has never been alone but yet always feels it because whoever he chooses to step out with isn't willing to go unless it's only in the way to satisfy them. Not caring for what helps him or willing to work with him; it's either their way or he is on his own. Thinking about his journey, he would always end up doing it the way to satisfy them, sacrificing what works and will help him. Looking up, asking God, why him? Why does he keep allowing himself to sacrifice for others knowing they are not willing to do the same for him? God speaks and reminds him everything is going to be okay. If nobody else has you, my son, I got you. So he relaxes, breathes, still scared. But he is willing to take the steps into his journey even if he has to do it alone.

"King & Queen"

Her glow is my light. Her love is my strength. Every moment in her presence, I feel like the greatest King ever. When I'm down, she lifts me up and pushes me to keep moving forward. When things go wrong, she lets me know she has my back and that we will get through it together. When she is down, I lift her up, letting her know I got her back no matter what motivates her to never stop moving forward because I'm going to be right there with her. We are a team, and nothing else matters because we are building our Empire as King and Queen. Outsiders can't destroy it. Understanding what we are trying to do and what's going on, we grind nonstop, no matter what it takes. I'm her King, and she is my Queen, and we are building this life for us, and together we control our happiness and where our lives take us as we continue to build and mold it the way we want it.

"Sipping Memories"

Sipping on this drink, I see your face.

That beautiful smile, that cute little laugh, that warm touch when we hold each other. Can't help but think about what we used to do. Loving every moment; seeing how happy you are every time I'm around. Damn, I need to put this drink down because the more I sip, the more I want you. Then again, that won't help because even with a sober mind, you're still there. Man, this is deep because when I'm with you, I feel I've found my soulmate. The long conversations, the laughter, the agreements to disagreements, but we agree more than we disagree. I can't lie to you because you're wonderful and I love it. My best friend and I love you. Every time I sip, it's like a replay of the moments we had and I just kick back and vibe. Relaxing to the memories, I sip and smile because I know just how wonderful you are.

"The Rose"

When you see her, you would have never known her heart has been broken. The strength she carries takes a strong man to handle it because a weak man she will destroy. The damage her past had done to her heart is like a rose that died. He was her water, her nutrients, her sun that kept her blooming. When he stripped it away, she died and lost her bloom. All she asked for was peace while she rebuilt herself to the Queen she knows she is. So as you see her now, she is her own water, her own nutrients, and as she blooms, it's like the sun is on her at all times. She is beautiful, inside and out. Even she knows it with her head held high as she handles her business and lives for herself. She promises never to allow another man tear her down. She won't let anyone take her bloom because everything she believes, she is, everything she knows she deserves, she truly deserves it all. She is a beautiful rose in and out. It was destroyed but now rebuilt within her own strength.

"A Little Conversation"

Hey, how are you? My name is Jimmy.

I'm not trying to be a bother; I just saw this

Beautiful specimen of a woman, which so happens to be you. I just wanted to have a little conversation if that's not too much to ask. If I'm doing too much, then just tell me, and I'll go away. I'm not trying to jump into a relationship or get into bed with you right away; just a little convo is okay with me. If I'm asking for too much again, I'll go away. I just want to talk and get to know you. Try to make you smile, maybe even get a chuckle out of you. Ha ha! I see that little slit smile I take is a yes. I'm getting a little somewhere, so let's start there and see where our conversation leads us, where life takes us. I'm not concerned about your past, but I'll sit and listen. I want to learn and understand where you come from. I'll explain mine so you will know where I've come from. Then we can go from there to move into the future. So I ask if it's not too much. Can I have this moment to take a little bit of your time for a little conversation?

"Have it all"

From the moment I walk in the room, I watch you light up. Your mood and atmosphere shift in my direction like waves in the ocean. Everything in you feels so right. With you in my presence, nothing else matters. When I'm with you, everything in me says I want it all. I know you want it too because I can see it in your face. Shining like the brightest star in the sky, you have me in a daze. As if I was high. Hearts singing out to each other, we want it all. See my arms and just fall, and I promise it won't hurt at all. Your amazement is so dear when I'm with you; it's like I have nothing to fear. Looking into my eyes, you know just what you want. I do too. I want you to feel me and understand me and know that I want it all. It's only you and I. That's why you rather keep me distant while we handle other things because together, everything else doesn't even matter anymore; everything feels so right. We can truly have it all.

"Expiration date"

The moment you think you're king because you think you have it all. Got your main woman at home cooking and cleaning, helping take care of home; then you have your little play toy on the side that you see from time to time, not thinking their paths will ever cross. You living it up; telling your boys about it, and they rocking with you like, yea bro, that's what's up, but be careful. So while you're out living it up thinking you got it made, your two pieces be at home thinking; main woman thinking, what could you really be doing with all your time because your time with her has become short. Then your little toy starts wondering could there ever be a chance she could be the main woman. Talking to both steadily making up new lies to tell to keep them apart but little do you know time is winding down. The more time you waste, the more lies you tell. And the more they get tired. Then it happens. They meet. They finally find out about each other. Now your mind is stuck, wondering what next. Heart racing, skipping, twitching because you don't know what to do; don't know which direction to go in. Should you stay or go? Guess what? You have now reached your expiration date.

—————— **66** ——————

Permission: now that you have reached the end, calm your mind and relax your soul and express your blissful moments.

—————— **99** ——————

CHAPTER 7

Stories

We all have stories in our life, good or bad. As you walk this journey into these stories, feel free to express your own. Understand that no one's story is greater than the other. Know that we all have our own stories, and it's up to us to decide how we allow those stories to shape us and determine how we move toward our future.

What is your story

From the time you wake till the moment you lay back down to rest, why do you live? Is it just to live in the moment? Taking it day by day just to maintain what you have? Or is it to live to be greater than you were the day before? Is it to live the same way you were brought up in this world from the time you were born, or is it to be greater than what you were brought up from? Why do you live? What is your story, and how will you write it? Is your story going to be about being greater than what you came from or still in the same script you were living since you were brought into this world? From the time you wake till the moment you lay back down to rest. What is your story?

One True Love, but She Can't See

It all started when I first saw her. She was the most beautiful girl I have ever seen; she shined like an angel. Every time I saw her or was around her, I would just get this crazy feeling inside. She never really knew me because I was always quiet. She got pregnant, and that's when I thought I had lost her. Years went by, and I finally started talking to her. We got together, and it has been hell ever since. I expressed how I felt. All I got back was lies and cheating more than once, but I forgave her and still loved her. It started with lies then moved on to cheating. She slept with a boy with the name of an animal. It happened more than once. Then she tried to talk to my brother, not thinking he would tell me. I broke up with her more than once, but I continued to take her back. I think she's making me soft cause this is just not me. I cried so much. She told me she cried to get me back and me loving her the way that I do; I did. She expressed herself to one of my brothers, but she was scared to do it for me. She doesn't believe anything I say, and all I do is sit back and cry.

If it doesn't get any better, I'm about to say forget it and stop crying. I really love her, but the way she is treating me and acting toward me, I'm starting to think she doesn't really love me or want to be with me like she keeps telling me she does. She needs to show me something. If she keeps doing me like she does and thinking everything I do or say is a lie, I'm just going to change my mind about marrying her. I'll just move on and cut her loose.

So Call Want To Be Wife

It all started when I asked her if there was anything that she wanted to tell me or ask me. The first thing she said is, "will I marry her?" I was stunned and amazed; I was just so happy. From that day, I knew we were meant to be together. I wanted everything to be perfect, but it was just not happening. We both were going through hard times. I had female problems, and it was breaking my baby's heart. She was breaking my heart too, but we fought through it. We just kept breaking up and getting back together off and on. If she wasn't breaking up with me, then I was breaking up with her. Not this time. I'm not losing my baby anymore. My goal is to marry her, and I will do it. My baby is moving away from me, but not too far. We will see each other again. Nothing is breaking us apart. She is my angel, and I'm not letting her go. We will get married, and that's on my life. She will be my wife. No matter what. I love her too much to ever let her go.

The Life I Went Through To Get My Love

Okay, here we go. Another week has gone by. I broke up with a girl that really didn't want me, got with a girl that really does want to be with me and lost a brother. I've liked this girl forever now, and she always liked me, but she wasn't ready to be in a relationship. I kept trying until another boy came into the picture. It didn't really slow me down because he already has a good girl. So she and I became closer and closer, but then another boy came into the picture, so it became two boys instead of one. That's when I thought my chances were shot. So I kind of slowed down some more but not too much because he had a good girl too. This girl came into my life telling me how she really likes me and has liked me for a long time but was too shy to tell me. So I started liking her and we got together. Not a good week goes by and she tells me that she doesn't know why she wants to be with me and why she really likes me. Then she tells me she doesn't really like me enough to have me as a boyfriend, so we broke up. A couple of days go by in the week, and the girl I've been trying to be with forever finally comes into my life, and we finally get together. I tell my brother about it and he gets mad after he tells me he doesn't even like her. Then later, my ex texts me asking me who I go with and I tell her, and she gets mad. I started to trip because I'm like, why is she getting mad when she told me that she didn't like me for a boyfriend and then lied about telling me she told me I would never have to worry about losing her? I didn't really start getting mad until I found out she said she lost interest in me after she told me she really liked me for a long time. Then I found out her and my brother were talking after he told me he wasn't going to go with her. Then I found out they had been liking each other for a long time and kept it from me until after we broke up. So we had our choice of words, then I lost my brother, and I got my true baby. I finally got my baby, and we were happily in love, and nothing was going to split us apart. We made a promise to each other to always be together no matter what and fight through the hard times to be together. Now we have to sit down and talk to her mom and explain everything to her because I love her mom and respect her.

The Happening

It all started when I first saw her. She lit up like a star, and all I could say was, "wow, she is beautiful." Me and my ex were on bad terms, so this beauty came into my life, and we hit it off great. We talked and spent a lot of time together, and we never had a problem. Our problems didn't start until I finally split from my ex, and she said she did the same. We started going together, and we were doing good, and we kept each other happy. We started to get deep feelings for each other; well, I did; she just spoke to me. Before it got any deeper, my ex brought it to my attention that the girl I'm with is still with her ex, so I left her alone. Weeks later, the girl came back to me saying that we could finally be official, so I took her back. We started off good again, then she started telling me how much she loves me and wants to have my son and marry me and all that, and I fell in love with her. Months went by, and then out of nowhere, her ex called me out of the blue telling me that he and the girl I'm with are still together, and he told me everything she said about how she was dissing me and stuff, so I left her alone again. Couple of weeks go by, and she comes back, and we get back together and the same thing happens. She tells me again she wants to marry me and have my son; I mean spitting at me hard, and I got deeper into her feeling the same way. So then I find out she has the same feelings for my homeboy, and she wants to be with him more and give her heart to him, and he doesn't even care for her. So I let her go to him. So we kept in touch as friends, but then she comes back to me talking about how she misses me and still loves me and wants my son and all that because she said the dude is nothing like me and she wants what I got back but yet I give her proof that the dude don't care for her, but she still runs back to him and stayed with him. So I just completely left it alone and threw it away. Now my ex has come back to me, and she is trying to make things right.

Stay My Angel

My heart pumps slowly. My mind is in wonder.
My soul leaves me. My body is down cold.
My halo is dem.

My soul found her, and I began to change. Her touch
uplifts me. Her kiss warms me. Her hands around my
heart and she combines it with hers, and my heart
flows steady, and my halo shines bright.

She takes my hands and gives me a kiss and says
we are together forever, your heart is safe with me.
Let's fly together so the whole world can see. Just
when I thought my wings were dead, her coming
into my life, they sat beautifully on my back
like a well groomed sheep.

She is my angel. I've sworn to keep as we fly through
this world for everyone to see. She brought me to life,
she is God's angel that I shall keep forever and hold on
tight long as she is willing to stay. She makes me
happy, I make her happy. I got on my knees to pray
and asked the Lord will she please stay.

Life of Loving You

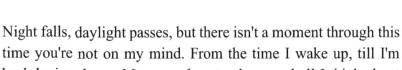

Night falls, daylight passes, but there isn't a moment through this time you're not on my mind. From the time I wake up, till I'm back laying down. My eyes close to sleep, and all I think about is you. You're there in my dreams. They feel so real I can't help but wake with a smile with only two things on my mind, you and wishing you were here.

To embrace your love, I will never do anything to hurt you but be there and protect you. Your heart, your love, your spirit, your mind, and body are so special to me, giving me it all; I will cherish them and take care of them forever. Your meaning to my life is the completion to my world, and nothing can stand in the way as long as you're willing to stand in this world with me. I want to be your completion to your world. The man you give your all to without holding anything back. Us together putting our worlds together is a ride worth me riding. I'm willing to live forever. To be there through pain and sickness, through your downs and outs, I will be that man that will always be there for you. Our love together conquers all and expressing all my love to you, there aren't enough words in the biggest book to express it all, but to express it by showing I can do each and every day you will have me and only me.

Watching

When I first saw her, my mind was like, "wow, she is beautiful."
I wanted to speak, but my mouth froze with fear of getting dissed.
Eyes glowing, leaving an image that I could never forget.
Watching guys step into her presence like a pack of wolves as I
sit back like a king, watching a woman stand so calm, and I'm
wondering if she will give me the chance to be her king. All these
thoughts in my head, but she is so beautiful I don't know what to
say because I don't want to say the wrong thing. I don't want to
seem anxious and make her mad, wanting her to be my Queen. I
don't want to rush either because of all the hurt and pain I've been
through, and I'm sure she has been hurt before too. Both mindsets
of when she speaks to me wondering if I am really a good guy
that wants to be with her or just wants to play her, and my mind
on is she really a good woman that can be my Queen or like the
others and just want to hurt and use me. All these thoughts in our
minds, so we take things slow and time will tell for us. As time
goes by and we continue to talk, all we can do is hope for the
best. Her beauty glows every time I think of her. All I see is her
from the time I wake up till the time I fall asleep; all I see is her.

Reborn

There was this king that had it all. He could go anywhere he wanted to go, do anything he wanted to do. Even though he had everything, there was one thing missing; a queen to share it with. So one day, he set out to find that queen he could share it all with. Searching high and low, he started to think he would never find her. Then one day, he set out to give it another go, and out of nowhere, he ran into this beautiful woman that stood so beautiful from head to toe; from the smoothness of her shiny silk hair to the beauty of her face all the way down to the perfect curves in her hips. Her beauty had him in a daze, and little did he know, her soul was about to send him straight to hell. He took her in and gave her everything she could ever want. Taking advantage of everything he did for her, she destroyed his soul in the process; disrespecting him every chance she got walking all over him till she took him for everything he had; then disappeared and he found himself down with the peasants with nothing but a dark soul and a cold heart. Peasants looking at him and calling him a fool and saying, how could you let a woman destroy you and take everything? Filled with so much pain, he disappeared for a while till he could get himself back together. With time going by, he took his dark soul and cold heart and was determined to get back to his king status and get back everything that was taken from him. Day in and day out, he worked and grinded his way back to the top. Every obstacle wasn't easy; some even set him back a couple of steps, but he didn't let it stop him. He was going to get back to the top. Through all his hard work, he had finally done it and was back at his king status but yet still no queen. As much as he wanted a queen, he no longer knew how to trust or believe anything a woman said. So feeling the way he felt, he didn't set out to find his queen; he just let time decide, and in the process, he just enjoyed being back on top. Then one day, his queen finally came, but at the moment, he didn't know she was his queen because he just saw her as another woman that he didn't trust; she was just beautiful. Her beauty didn't mean anything to him, but her spirit and how she treated him is what kept him around. Through communication and understanding, she learned just how damaged he was, and instead of walking away, she was patient, soothing, peaceful, caring, and motivating, and didn't ask him for anything other than helping himself get out of that dark, cold place his soul and heart was in and be that loving king she felt and knew he could be. Each day his soul got brighter; each day, his heart got warmer, melting the ice around his heart. She had completely helped him out of that dark, cold place because even in the dark, he showed her the light in him and that the dark did not completely take control of him. He just used it to get back on top, and once she helped him get his light back, she became his queen, and together they built the biggest empire that he couldn't even have imagined, and he was so happy it was like he had been reborn and now has everything he ever wanted plus more with his queen right by his side.

Feeling Like You're Alone

The dream to make it isn't easy. Striving for something you believe in, not just for yourself, but for your family also. The struggle is real, and wanting to get out is not easy when you're finding yourself helping and supporting others and you look around, trying to find who is helping you. Who's supporting you? Sometimes it gets to the point where you want to stop helping others and supporting others because when you look around, they are not doing the same for you. As a man, you try to stay strong and focused and motivate yourself to keep moving forward, but sometimes you need somebody in your corner helping you, supporting you, motivating you, and believing in you. It's good to know your mother is there trying to do those things, but you still would like to have someone by your side other than your mother. Like actually having a real woman beside you, supporting you, helping you, motivating you, and pushing you and always by your side no matter what, through anything, because she believes in you and knows you will do the same for her. Actually, having your true friends be there for you; helping you, supporting you, pushing you, motivating you, and believing in you and not just sitting around asking for your help and you got to push them and try to motivate them and try to believe in them, but they don't do the same for you because if you don't do something, they won't do it nor try to push you or motivate you to do it. Being a leader is good and all, but even a leader needs a little help, motivation, push, and belief. You ask for these things, but yet you look around and find yourself standing alone every time, just you, your mother, and God. No woman by your side helping others and your friends but nothing in return, and if you don't do something, they don't do it either, and there is no motivation, no push. They say God is all you need and everything will be okay, but even God has a woman by His side. He died for our sins, but He still has people believing in Him. The life of trying to make it and chasing your dream to do what you love and live comfortably will never be easy, and being self-motivated will still have you needing someone there with you, believing in you, motivating you, pushing you, and helping you. With the way this world is, it's hard trying to make it by yourself with no help and no one really by your side because you need it, and it makes things better and helpful and a little less stressful.

— 66 —

Permission: Now that you have reached the end, calm your mind and relax your soul and feel free to express your self

— 99 —

CHAPTER 8

Spiritual

The spiritual journey you are about to embark on gives you the permission to express your spirituality no matter what you believe or who you believe in. Express your spirituality and feel free to let go and calm your soul. Staying spiritually grounded is necessary because the people who come into our lives can cause us to wonder if they are good or bad; if they are Angels or Demons.

The Angel that Walks in Silence

She is an angel that lights up the room when she walks.

She has a smile that's so bright, she walks without fright. She is so quiet that you barely hear her but her beauty is like a beautiful white rabbit hopping among mixed breeds.

She walks and talks with silence. Like a little mouse scattering through your house and once you see it you can't help but stop in your tracks.

She is peaceful, but she shines like a beautiful angel that floats with a glow.

My Angel

My Angel! My Angel!

I flew the day and night skies looking for her.
She finally flew in my sight, and I have been after
her ever since. We became friends for a long time till
we felt a special connection that we should be together.
We started getting close, but she was not ready to
make it be real because she had been hurt. I talked
and talked, but I couldn't bring her to a halt.
She finally realized she wanted me,
and we've been working on it ever since.

The Lord's Angel

I cried; I shivered. I lied; I died.
I lost my soul, but it wasn't as bad as
I'd thought it would be.
It left my body and took off to the heavens. It came
back with a surprise; I woke up with a new hide.
I walk the earth with a sense of pride and with
beautiful white wings never with my head
down in the sense of side.
I have been reborn up under the Lord's Prayer; I am
the Lord's angel, and I'm living life to the fullest.

Seeking for Help

My life is gone.
The devil comes out.
He takes my soul; I look down and become puzzled.
I'm lost within the earth; nowhere to be found.
Lord, seek out my soul.
Bring me back to life.
Make me your angel, and I shall be crowned.

Finally Got My Angel

Lord O' Lord, you sent me my angel, and I truly thank you. She was right up under my nose this whole time, but my eyes were nearly closed. She finally got her digital; that's when we started getting physical. She would skip around in the book but still had me on every page she looked at. We talked all night and didn't have one fight. She told me how long she had liked me, and at one point, I broke her heart. I never knew then how she felt because we never really talked, and I did something I never meant to do. I wouldn't have done it if she would have at least thrown me a hint. Now I finally got her. I was sorry and it will never happen again and that's what I meant. We are living a secret relationship happily as ever but waiting for the time it can come out.

Listen To the Word

You can hear the word. You can see the word. You can also feel the word, but it's your choice to carry out the word. I've bounced from church to church hearing the word, but I could never understand it. So I went through churches with devils in the middle of what was supposed to be the house of god. As I tried to listen to God, I thought the church was a fraud. I left church and talked to God in my room. My mom came to me and said you will be able to go back to church soon. We found a church in the woods, and as I was there, I found my brother from my hood. I sat through church, and as days passed, the more I heard the word, my life began to change. I sat at a table with my mom and heard her talk. I actually could understand the words she spoke that day.

I Died, but Through Her, I Live.

I had this dream, and in this dream, I died. I don't know how, when, or where I was; I was just dead. Nobody could see me but two people. That was my mom and the one I love. My soul wanders the earth, and nobody can talk to me but these two. Around my mom, she can see me and talk to me, and we talk all the time, but when I'm with my love, I am alive. I have flesh, bones, and blood flow and everything. I can feel her and she can feel me. It's like I'm walking this earth, and the only time I'm truly alive is when I'm with her. She is my life and without her, my soul runs free. Away from her, I am dead, but with her, I'm completely alive, living happily as ever.

"

Permission: now that you have reached the end, calm your mind and relax your soul and express your spiritual realm.

"

Conclusion

At a moment in my life, this all started as just a game of who could write the best. Eventually that evolved into me really putting it into a book and releasing those emotions on paper. The more I wrote the more it kept coming into my mind to actually publish it. Being pushed by my brother inspired me to get it done. Talking around with other people also gave me that motivation to really put it out there because I wasn't the only one that struggled with expressing himself. There are a lot of men in this world that struggle to do the same. For a long time, man has walked this earth, and it has been one of the biggest struggles, especially for men who fear expressing themselves without being looked at as weak or soft. Now that you've gone through this book and have reached the end, I hope you feel the freedom to express yourself in any way possible. If you're not at a place in your life where you can speak it out loud then put it down on paper. If you don't feel like writing then type it. If you don't feel like writing or typing then record yourself, but whatever you do, don't hold it in; release your emotions anyway possible.

Feel free to reach out to me and contact me on any of my social sites. You are not alone in the struggle of expression. I hope after you read through this book, it helps you get closer to your freedom and get comfortable with releasing and expressing your emotions.